One man's trash is another man's treasure.

This logbook belongs to

_____

copyright 2019 Owthorne Notebooks

Today's Sales

Today's date: _____

Cost of stall/materials: _____

Total float money brought: _____

Item sold	Sold for	Bought for	Location	Profit

Item sold	Sold for	Bought for	Location	Profit

Today's total takings: _____

Today's total profit: _____

Today's best seller: _____

Today's Sales

Today's date: _____
Cost of stall/materials: _____
Total float money brought: _____

Item sold	Sold for	Bought for	Location	Profit

Item sold	Sold for	Bought for	Location	Profit

Today's total takings: _____

Today's total profit: _____

Today's best seller: _____

Today's Sales

Today's date: _____
Cost of stall/materials: _____
Total float money brought: _____

Item sold	Sold for	Bought for	Location	Profit

Item sold	Sold for	Bought for	Location	Profit

Today's total takings: _____

Today's total profit: _____

Today's best seller: _____

Today's Sales

Today's date: _____
Cost of stall/materials: _____
Total float money brought: _____

Item sold	Sold for	Bought for	Location	Profit

Item sold	Sold for	Bought for	Location	Profit

Today's total takings: _____

Today's total profit: _____

Today's best seller: _____

Today's Sales

Today's date: _____
Cost of stall/materials: _____
Total float money brought: _____

Item sold	Sold for	Bought for	Location	Profit

Item sold	Sold for	Bought for	Location	Profit

Today's total takings: _____

Today's total profit: _____

Today's best seller: _____

Today's Sales

Today's date: _____
Cost of stall/materials: _____
Total float money brought: _____

Item sold	Sold for	Bought for	Location	Profit

Item sold	Sold for	Bought for	Location	Profit

Today's total takings: _____

Today's total profit: _____

Today's best seller: _____

Today's sales

Today's date: _____
Cost of stall/materials: _____
Total float money brought: _____

Item sold	Sold for	Bought for	Location	Profit

Item sold	Sold for	Bought for	Location	Profit

Today's total takings: _____

Today's total profit: _____

Today's best seller: _____

Today's Sales

Today's date: _____
Cost of stall/materials: _____
Total float money brought: _____

Item sold	Sold for	Bought for	Location	Profit

Item sold	Sold for	Bought for	Location	Profit

Today's total takings: _____

Today's total profit: _____

Today's best seller: _____

Today's Sales

Today's date: _____

Cost of stall/materials: _____

Total float money brought: _____

Item sold	Sold for	Bought for	Location	Profit

Item sold	Sold for	Bought for	Location	Profit

Today's total takings: _____

Today's total profit: _____

Today's best seller: _____

Today's Sales

Today's date: _____
Cost of stall/materials: _____
Total float money brought: _____

Item sold	Sold for	Bought for	Location	Profit

Item sold	Sold for	Bought for	Location	Profit

Today's total takings: _____

Today's total profit: _____

Today's best seller: _____

Today's Sales

Today's date: _____

Cost of stall/materials: _____

Total float money brought: _____

Item sold	sold for	Bought for	Location	Profit

Item sold	Sold for	Bought for	Location	Profit

Today's total takings: _____

Today's total profit: _____

Today's best seller: _____

Today's Sales

Today's date: _____
Cost of stall/materials: _____
Total float money brought: _____

Item sold	Sold for	Bought for	Location	Profit

Item sold	Sold for	Bought for	Location	Profit

Today's total takings: _____

Today's total profit: _____

Today's best seller: _____

Today's Sales

Today's date: _____
Cost of stall/materials: _____
Total float money brought: _____

Item sold	Sold for	Bought for	Location	Profit

Item sold	Sold for	Bought for	Location	Profit

Today's total takings: _____

Today's total profit: _____

Today's best seller: _____

Today's Sales

Today's date: _____

Cost of stall/materials: _____

Total float money brought: _____

Item sold	Sold for	Bought for	Location	Profit

Item sold	Sold for	Bought for	Location	Profit

Today's total takings: _____

Today's total profit: _____

Today's best seller: _____

Today's Sales

Today's date: _____
Cost of stall/materials: _____
Total float money brought: _____

Item sold	Sold for	Bought for	Location	Profit

Item sold	Sold for	Bought for	Location	Profit

Today's total takings: _____

Today's total profit: _____

Today's best seller: _____

Today's Sales

Today's date: _____
Cost of stall/materials: _____
Total float money brought: _____

Item sold	Sold for	Bought for	Location	Profit

Item sold	Sold for	Bought for	Location	Profit

Today's total takings: _____

Today's total profit: _____

Today's best seller: _____

Today's Sales

Today's date: _____
Cost of stall/materials: _____
Total float money brought: _____

Item sold	Sold for	Bought for	Location	Profit

Item sold	Sold for	Bought for	Location	Profit

Today's total takings: _____

Today's total profit: _____

Today's best seller: _____

Today's Sales

Today's date: _____
Cost of stall/materials: _____
Total float money brought: _____

Item sold	Sold for	Bought for	Location	Profit

Item sold	Sold for	Bought for	Location	Profit

Today's total takings: _____

Today's total profit: _____

Today's best seller: _____

Today's sales

Today's date: _____

Cost of stall/materials: _____

Total float money brought: _____

Item sold	Sold for	Bought for	Location	Profit

Item sold	Sold for	Bought for	Location	Profit

Today's total takings: _____

Today's total profit: _____

Today's best seller: _____

Today's Sales

Today's date: _____

Cost of stall/materials: _____

Total float money brought: _____

Item sold	Sold for	Bought for	Location	Profit

Item sold	Sold for	Bought for	Location	Profit

Today's total takings: _____

Today's total profit: _____

Today's best seller: _____

Today's Sales

Today's date: _____
Cost of stall/materials: _____
Total float money brought: _____

Item sold	Sold for	Bought for	Location	Profit

Item sold	Sold for	Bought for	Location	Profit

Today's total takings: _____

Today's total profit: _____

Today's best seller: _____

Today's Sales

Today's date: _____

Cost of stall/materials: _____

Total float money brought: _____

Item sold	sold for	Bought for	Location	Profit

Item sold	Sold for	Bought for	Location	Profit

Today's total takings: _____

Today's total profit: _____

Today's best seller: _____

Today's Sales

Today's date: _____
Cost of stall/materials: _____
Total float money brought: _____

Item sold	Sold for	Bought for	Location	Profit

Item sold	Sold for	Bought for	Location	Profit

Today's total takings: _____

Today's total profit: _____

Today's best seller: _____

Today's Sales

Today's date: _____
Cost of stall/materials: _____
Total float money brought: _____

Item sold	sold for	Bought for	Location	Profit

Item sold	Sold for	Bought for	Location	Profit

Today's total takings: _____

Today's total profit: _____

Today's best seller: _____

Today's Sales

Today's date: _____
Cost of stall/materials: _____
Total float money brought: _____

Item sold	sold for	Bought for	Location	Profit

Item sold	Sold for	Bought for	Location	Profit

Today's total takings: _____

Today's total profit: _____

Today's best seller: _____

Today's Sales

Today's date: _____
Cost of stall/materials: _____
Total float money brought: _____

Item sold	Sold for	Bought for	Location	Profit

Item sold	Sold for	Bought for	Location	Profit

Today's total takings: _____

Today's total profit: _____

Today's best seller: _____

Today's Sales

Today's date: _____
Cost of stall/materials: _____
Total float money brought: _____

Item sold	sold for	Bought for	Location	Profit

Item sold	Sold for	Bought for	Location	Profit

Today's total takings: _____

Today's total profit: _____

Today's best seller: _____

Today's Sales

Today's date: _____
Cost of stall/materials: _____
Total float money brought: _____

Item sold	Sold for	Bought for	Location	Profit

Item sold	Sold for	Bought for	Location	Profit

Today's total takings: _____

Today's total profit: _____

Today's best seller: _____

Today's Sales

Today's date: _____

Cost of stall/materials: _____

Total float money brought: _____

Item sold	Sold for	Bought for	Location	Profit

Item sold	Sold for	Bought for	Location	Profit

Today's total takings: _____

Today's total profit: _____

Today's best seller: _____

Today's sales

Today's date: _____
Cost of stall/materials: _____
Total float money brought: _____

Item sold	Sold for	Bought for	Location	Profit

Item sold	Sold for	Bought for	Location	Profit

Today's total takings: _____

Today's total profit: _____

Today's best seller: _____

Today's Sales

Today's date: _____
Cost of stall/materials: _____
Total float money brought: _____

Item sold	sold for	Bought for	Location	Profit

Item sold	Sold for	Bought for	Location	Profit

Today's total takings: _____

Today's total profit: _____

Today's best seller: _____

Today's Sales

Today's date: _____

Cost of stall/materials: _____

Total float money brought: _____

Item sold	sold for	Bought for	Location	Profit

Item sold	Sold for	Bought for	Location	Profit

Today's total takings: _____

Today's total profit: _____

Today's best seller: _____

Today's Sales

Today's date: _____
Cost of stall/materials: _____
Total float money brought: _____

Item sold	sold for	Bought for	Location	Profit

Item sold	Sold for	Bought for	Location	Profit

Today's total takings: _____

Today's total profit: _____

Today's best seller: _____

Today's Sales

Today's date: _____

Cost of stall/materials: _____

Total float money brought: _____

Item sold	Sold for	Bought for	Location	Profit

Item sold	Sold for	Bought for	Location	Profit

Today's total takings: _____

Today's total profit: _____

Today's best seller: _____

Today's sales

Today's date: _____
Cost of stall/materials: _____
Total float money brought: _____

Item sold	Sold for	Bought for	Location	Profit

Item sold	Sold for	Bought for	Location	Profit

Today's total takings: _____

Today's total profit: _____

Today's best seller: _____

Today's Sales

Today's date: _____
Cost of stall/materials: _____
Total float money brought: _____

Item sold	sold for	Bought for	Location	Profit

Item sold	Sold for	Bought for	Location	Profit

Today's total takings: _____

Today's total profit: _____

Today's best seller: _____

Today's Sales

Today's date: _____
Cost of stall/materials: _____
Total float money brought: _____

Item sold	sold for	Bought for	Location	Profit

Item sold	Sold for	Bought for	Location	Profit

Today's total takings: _____

Today's total profit: _____

Today's best seller: _____

Today's Sales

Today's date: _____
Cost of stall/materials: _____
Total float money brought: _____

Item sold	Sold for	Bought for	Location	Profit

Item sold	Sold for	Bought for	Location	Profit

Today's total takings: _____

Today's total profit: _____

Today's best seller: _____

Today's Sales

Today's date: _____
Cost of stall/materials: _____
Total float money brought: _____

Item sold	sold for	Bought for	Location	Profit

Item sold	Sold for	Bought for	Location	Profit

Today's total takings: _____

Today's total profit: _____

Today's best seller: _____

Today's Sales

Today's date: _____

Cost of stall/materials: _____

Total float money brought: _____

Item sold	Sold for	Bought for	Location	Profit

Item sold	Sold for	Bought for	Location	Profit

Today's total takings:

Today's total profit:

Today's best seller:

Today's Sales

Today's date: _____
Cost of stall/materials: _____
Total float money brought: _____

Item sold	Sold for	Bought for	Location	Profit

Item sold	Sold for	Bought for	Location	Profit

Today's total takings: _____

Today's total profit: _____

Today's best seller: _____

Today's Sales

Today's date: _____

Cost of stall/materials: _____

Total float money brought: _____

Item sold	Sold for	Bought for	Location	Profit

Item sold	Sold for	Bought for	Location	Profit

Today's total takings: _____

Today's total profit: _____

Today's best seller: _____

Today's Sales

Today's date: _____
Cost of stall/materials: _____
Total float money brought: _____

Item sold	Sold for	Bought for	Location	Profit

Item sold	Sold for	Bought for	Location	Profit

Today's total takings: _____

Today's total profit: _____

Today's best seller: _____

Today's Sales

Today's date: _____

Cost of stall/materials: _____

Total float money brought: _____

Item sold	Sold for	Bought for	Location	Profit

Item sold	Sold for	Bought for	Location	Profit

Today's total takings: _____

Today's total profit: _____

Today's best seller: _____

Today's Sales

Today's date: _____

Cost of stall/materials: _____

Total float money brought: _____

Item sold	Sold for	Bought for	Location	Profit

Item sold	Sold for	Bought for	Location	Profit

Today's total takings:

Today's total profit:

Today's best seller:

Today's Sales

Today's date: _____
Cost of stall/materials: _____
Total float money brought: _____

Item sold	Sold for	Bought for	Location	Profit

Item sold	Sold for	Bought for	Location	Profit

Today's total takings: _____

Today's total profit: _____

Today's best seller: _____

Today's Sales

Today's date: _____
Cost of stall/materials: _____
Total float money brought: _____

Item sold	sold for	Bought for	Location	Profit

Item sold	Sold for	Bought for	Location	Profit

Today's total takings: _____

Today's total profit: _____

Today's best seller: _____

Today's Sales

Today's date: _____

Cost of stall/materials: _____

Total float money brought: _____

Item sold	Sold for	Bought for	Location	Profit

Item sold	Sold for	Bought for	Location	Profit

Today's total takings: _____

Today's total profit: _____

Today's best seller: _____

Today's Sales

Today's date: _____
Cost of stall/materials: _____
Total float money brought: _____

Item sold	sold for	Bought for	Location	Profit

Item sold	Sold for	Bought for	Location	Profit

Today's total takings: _____

Today's total profit: _____

Today's best seller: _____

Today's Sales

Today's date: _____
Cost of stall/materials: _____
Total float money brought: _____

Item sold	Sold for	Bought for	Location	Profit

Item sold	Sold for	Bought for	Location	Profit

Today's total takings: _____

Today's total profit: _____

Today's best seller: _____

Today's Sales

Today's date: _____

Cost of stall/materials: _____

Total float money brought: _____

Item sold	Sold for	Bought for	Location	Profit

Item sold	Sold for	Bought for	Location	Profit

Today's total takings: _____

Today's total profit: _____

Today's best seller: _____

Today's Sales

Today's date: _____
Cost of stall/materials: _____
Total float money brought: _____

Item sold	Sold for	Bought for	Location	Profit

Item sold	Sold for	Bought for	Location	Profit

Today's total takings: _____

Today's total profit: _____

Today's best seller: _____

Today's Sales

Today's date: _____
Cost of stall/materials: _____
Total float money brought: _____

Item sold	Sold for	Bought for	Location	Profit

Item sold	Sold for	Bought for	Location	Profit

Today's total takings: _____

Today's total profit: _____

Today's best seller: _____

Today's Sales

Today's date: _____

Cost of stall/materials: _____

Total float money brought: _____

Item sold	sold for	Bought for	Location	Profit

Item sold	Sold for	Bought for	Location	Profit

Today's total takings: _____

Today's total profit: _____

Today's best seller: _____

Today's Sales

Today's date: _____
Cost of stall/materials: _____
Total float money brought: _____

Item sold	Sold for	Bought for	Location	Profit

Item sold	Sold for	Bought for	Location	Profit

Today's total takings: _____

Today's total profit: _____

Today's best seller: _____

Today's Sales

Today's date: _____
Cost of stall/materials: _____
Total float money brought: _____

Item sold	sold for	Bought for	Location	Profit

Item sold	Sold for	Bought for	Location	Profit

Today's total takings: _____

Today's total profit: _____

Today's best seller: _____

Today's Sales

Today's date: _____

Cost of stall/materials: _____

Total float money brought: _____

Item sold	Sold for	Bought for	Location	Profit

Item sold	Sold for	Bought for	Location	Profit

Today's total takings: _____

Today's total profit: _____

Today's best seller: _____

Today's Sales

Today's date: _____
Cost of stall/materials: _____
Total float money brought: _____

Item sold	sold for	Bought for	Location	Profit

Item sold	Sold for	Bought for	Location	Profit

Today's total takings: _____

Today's total profit: _____

Today's best seller: _____

Today's Sales

Today's date: _____
Cost of stall/materials: _____
Total float money brought: _____

Item sold	Sold for	Bought for	Location	Profit

Item sold	Sold for	Bought for	Location	Profit

Today's total takings: _____

Today's total profit: _____

Today's best seller: _____

One man's trash is another man's treasure.

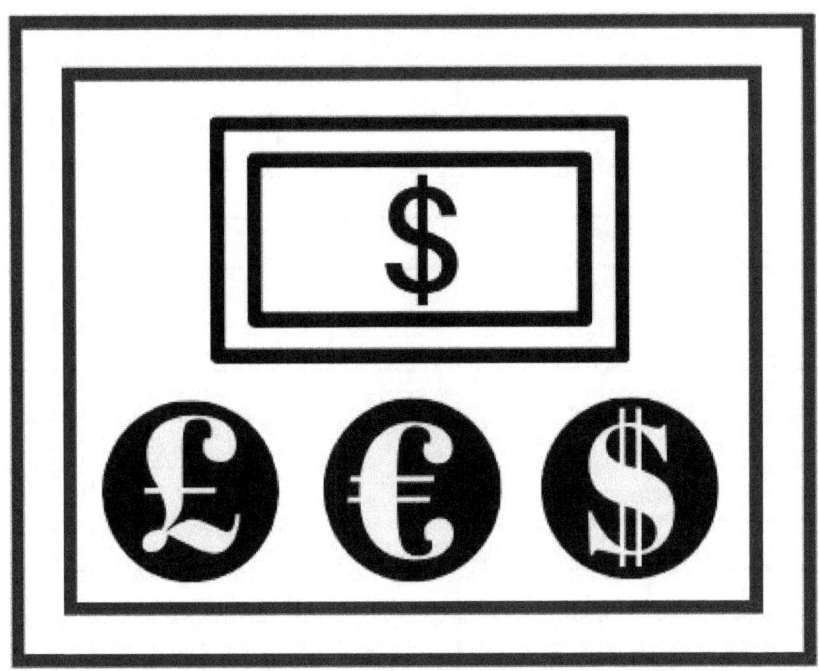

copyright 2019 Owthorne Notebooks

www.ingramcontent.com/pod-product-compliance
Lightning Source LLC
Chambersburg PA
CBHW072213170526
45158CB00002BA/575